AHHHH
I'M SO BORED!

Activity Book For Teens

Made by Teens

INSTRUCTIONS

Make a mess of this book!

Play with your friends or alone to pass the time.

Each game has individual instructions.

Solutions to puzzles in the back of the book

Most of all have some fun!

MASH

M.A.S.H. is a fortune telling game.
The name comes from the words: Mansion, Apartment, Shack, House.

1. List four or five options for each category with picking a terrible last option for each. This is a special holiday vacation edition so think about what your holiday could be like good or bad.

2. You can have a friend draw a spiral in the dedicated circle or if you are alone, close your eyes while you draw your spiral. Randomly stop and count the number of spiral lines. This number will be your magic number you can put in the heart.

3. Count through each of the categories until you reach the magic number. Start from the M at the top and moving clockwise counting each option until you reach the magic number. Cross of the options you have landed on until you reach one remaining option. Do this for each category leaving one for each.

4. Read each category revealing your fortune!

CATEGORIES PAPER GAME

In this game you have to try to find words in different categories starting with the same letter and beat your rivals.

Use dice to count through the alphabet for a letter or pick one at random.

DOTS AND BOXES

The goal is to own as many squares/boxes as possible. Two players take turns one by one making a line connecting dots with only vertical and horizontal lines. If a player completes the fourth side of a box then he/she has to write his/her initials in the box and then takes an extra turn.

Who ever completes the most boxes wins!

M.A.S.H.

MANSION-APARTMENT-SHACK-HOUSE

Future Spouse

1. _____
2. _____
3. _____
4. _____
5. _____

Future Pets

1. _____
2. _____
3. _____
4. _____
5. _____

Future Car

1. _____
2. _____
3. _____
4. _____
5. _____

Future Job

1. _____
2. _____
3. _____
4. _____
5. _____

Number of Kids

1. _____
2. _____
3. _____
4. _____
5. _____

Future City

1. _____
2. _____
3. _____
4. _____
5. _____

Spiral Circle

Your Magic Number

CATEGORIES GAME

Letter	Country	Animal	Name	Job	City	Score

Number of Rounds	Total Score

DOTS AND BOXES

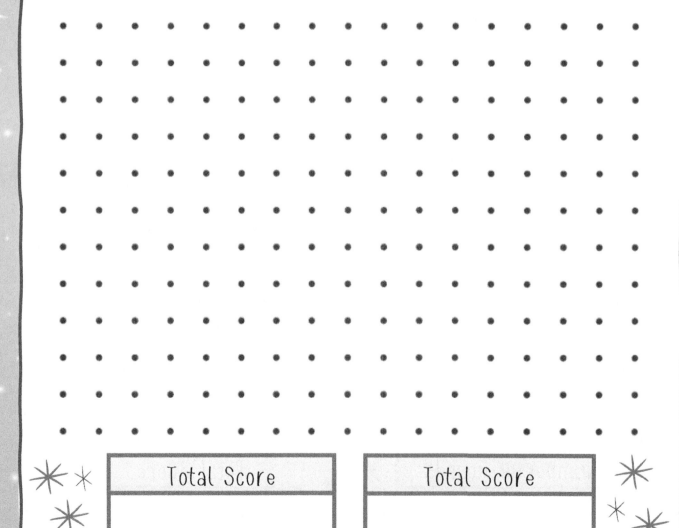

Total Score	Total Score

3D WEAVE MAZE #1

Start

Finish

FREE DRAW

Draw your favorite food.

M.A.S.H.

MANSION-APARTMENT-SHACK-HOUSE

Future Spouse

1. _____
2. _____
3. _____
4. _____
5. _____

Future Pets

1. _____
2. _____
3. _____
4. _____
5. _____

Future Car

1. _____
2. _____
3. _____
4. _____
5. _____

Future Job

1. _____
2. _____
3. _____
4. _____
5. _____

Number of Kids

1. _____
2. _____
3. _____
4. _____
5. _____

Future City

1. _____
2. _____
3. _____
4. _____
5. _____

Spiral Circle

Your Magic Number

CATEGORIES GAME

Letter	Country	Animal	Name	Job	City	Score

Number of Rounds

Total Score

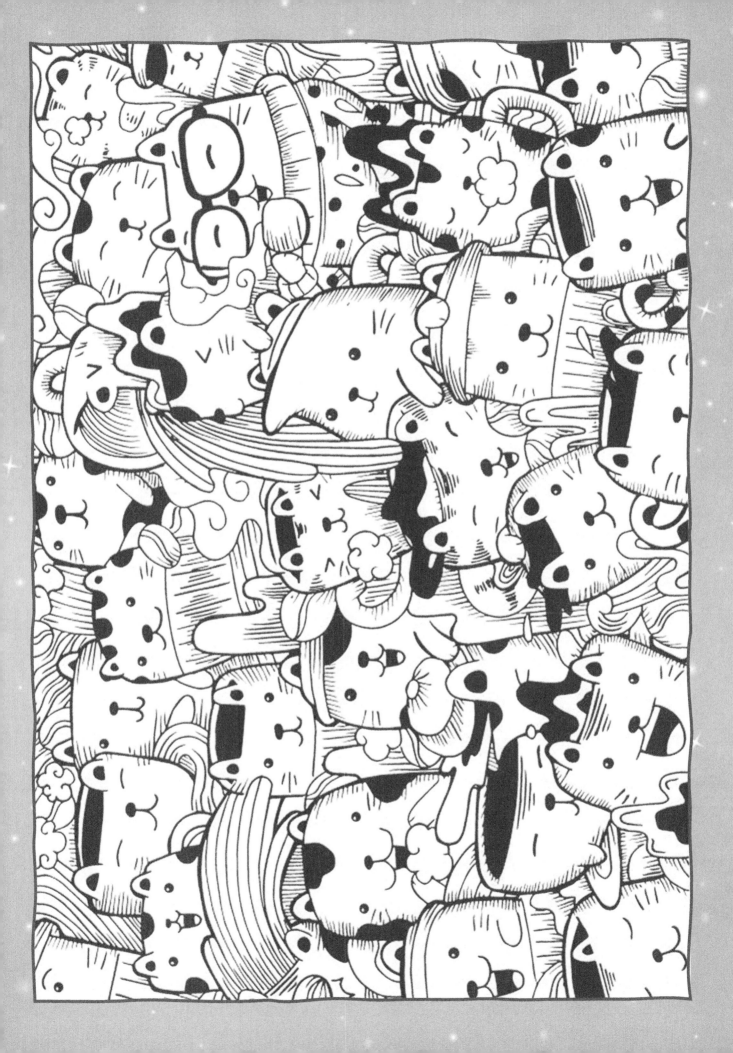

EASY

DOTS AND BOXES

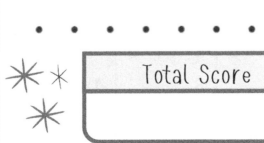

Total Score

Total Score

FREE DRAW

Draw biggest fear.

M.A.S.H.

MANSION–APARTMENT–SHACK–HOUSE

Future Spouse

1. _____
2. _____
3. _____
4. _____
5. _____

Future Pets

1. _____
2. _____
3. _____
4. _____
5. _____

Future Car

1. _____
2. _____
3. _____
4. _____
5. _____

Future Job

1. _____
2. _____
3. _____
4. _____
5. _____

Number of Kids

1. _____
2. _____
3. _____
4. _____
5. _____

Future City

1. _____
2. _____
3. _____
4. _____
5. _____

Spiral Circle

Your Magic Number

CATEGORIES GAME

Letter	Country	Animal	Name	Job	City	Score

Number of Rounds

Total Score

DOTS AND BOXES

Total Score

Total Score

3D WEAVE MAZE #2

Start

Finish

FREE DRAW

Draw yourself.

M.A.S.H.

MANSION-APARTMENT-SHACK-HOUSE

Future Spouse

1. _____
2. _____
3. _____
4. _____
5. _____

Future Pets

1. _____
2. _____
3. _____
4. _____
5. _____

Future Car

1. _____
2. _____
3. _____
4. _____
5. _____

Future Job

1. _____
2. _____
3. _____
4. _____
5. _____

Number of Kids

1. _____
2. _____
3. _____
4. _____
5. _____

Future City

1. _____
2. _____
3. _____
4. _____
5. _____

Spiral Circle

Your Magic Number

CATEGORIES GAME

Letter	Country	Animal	Name	Job	City	Score

Number of Rounds

Total Score

DOTS AND BOXES

Total Score

Total Score

M.A.S.H.

MANSION-APARTMENT-SHACK-HOUSE

Future Spouse

1. _____
2. _____
3. _____
4. _____
5. _____

Future Pets

1. _____
2. _____
3. _____
4. _____
5. _____

Future Car

1. _____
2. _____
3. _____
4. _____
5. _____

Future Job

1. _____
2. _____
3. _____
4. _____
5. _____

Number of Kids

1. _____
2. _____
3. _____
4. _____
5. _____

Future City

1. _____
2. _____
3. _____
4. _____
5. _____

Spiral Circle

Your Magic Number

FREE DRAW

Draw your dream vacation spot.

3D WEAVE MAZE #3

Start

Finish

CATEGORIES GAME

Letter	Country	Animal	Name	Job	City	Score

Number of Rounds		Total Score

DOTS AND BOXES

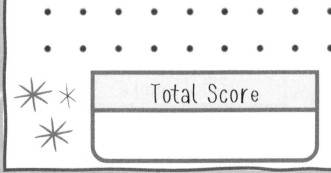

Total Score

Total Score

FREE DRAW

Draw your favorite activity.

M.A.S.H.

MANSION-APARTMENT-SHACK-HOUSE

Future Spouse
1. _____
2. _____
3. _____
4. _____
5. _____

Future Pets
1. _____
2. _____
3. _____
4. _____
5. _____

Future Car
1. _____
2. _____
3. _____
4. _____
5. _____

Future Job
1. _____
2. _____
3. _____
4. _____
5. _____

Number of Kids
1. _____
2. _____
3. _____
4. _____
5. _____

Future City
1. _____
2. _____
3. _____
4. _____
5. _____

Spiral Circle

Your Magic Number

CATEGORIES GAME

Letter	Country	Animal	Name	Job	City	Score

Number of Rounds	Total Score

M.A.S.H.

MANSION-APARTMENT-SHACK-HOUSE

Future Spouse

1. _____
2. _____
3. _____
4. _____
5. _____

Future Pets

1. _____
2. _____
3. _____
4. _____
5. _____

Future Car

1. _____
2. _____
3. _____
4. _____
5. _____

Future Job

1. _____
2. _____
3. _____
4. _____
5. _____

Number of Kids

1. _____
2. _____
3. _____
4. _____
5. _____

Future City

1. _____
2. _____
3. _____
4. _____
5. _____

Spiral Circle

Your Magic Number

DOTS AND BOXES

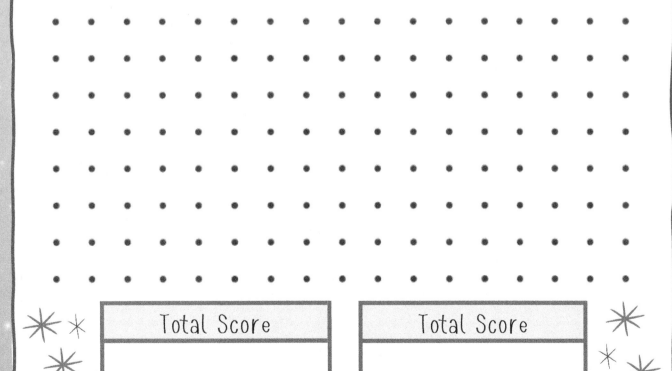

Total Score

Total Score

FREE DRAW

Draw your family.

M.A.S.H.

MANSION-APARTMENT- SHACK-HOUSE

Future Spouse

1. _____
2. _____
3. _____
4. _____
5. _____

Future Pets

1. _____
2. _____
3. _____
4. _____
5. _____

Future Car

1. _____
2. _____
3. _____
4. _____
5. _____

Future Job

1. _____
2. _____
3. _____
4. _____
5. _____

Number of Kids

1. _____
2. _____
3. _____
4. _____
5. _____

Future City

1. _____
2. _____
3. _____
4. _____
5. _____

Spiral Circle

Your Magic Number

CATEGORIES GAME

Letter	Country	Animal	Name	Job	City	Score

Number of Rounds

Total Score

 # MEDIUM

Puzzle 1

		3	6	9	4			
6		5					8	
		4			5			
4	9	1			2	6	7	8
3		7	4			1		5
		2	6	7	1	3	9	4
	5	6	9		3			
	7	3	8	5	4	2	6	9
8	4		7				3	1

Puzzle 2

9	4		1	6	8	7		
5			2	3				6
2	6		5		4		8	9
8		5	6		2			
	2	9	4	1			6	5
6	3		7	8		9	2	1
	9		8	5	7	2	1	
4			3	2	1		9	
			9		6		3	7

Puzzle 3

9	6					2		1
			9	6	2		5	7
8		2		1	7			
2				7	4	6		
	4	6	1			9		7
7	3	8	6	9	5	4		
1		3		6		7		9
6	7	5		3		1		4
4			7		1			

Puzzle 4

2	6	7	5			8		
9	5	3	2		4	1	7	6
						2		5
			6	2		3		7
					1	9		8
6			3	5	9	4		2
5	8	2				7	4	3
7			4		3			1
		3	6	7	4	2	5	

DOTS AND BOXES

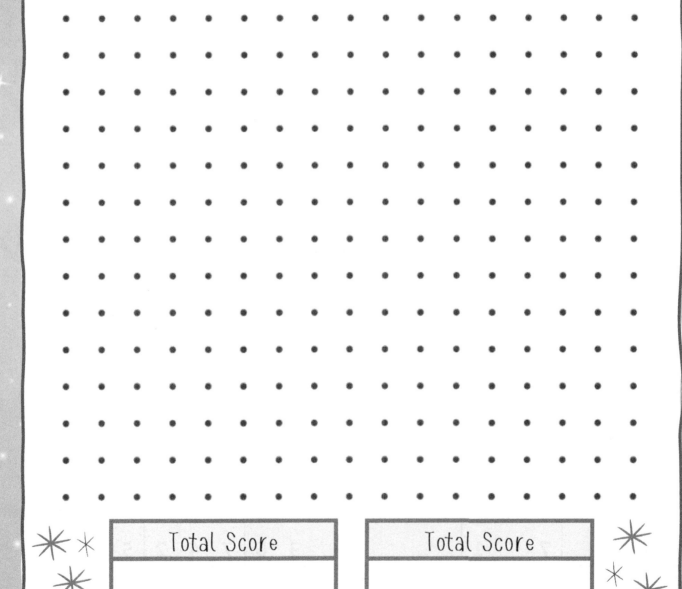

Total Score

Total Score

FREE DRAW

Draw your favorite people.

M.A.S.H.

MANSION-APARTMENT-SHACK-HOUSE

Future Spouse

1. _____
2. _____
3. _____
4. _____
5. _____

Future Pets

1. _____
2. _____
3. _____
4. _____
5. _____

Future Car

1. _____
2. _____
3. _____
4. _____
5. _____

Future Job

1. _____
2. _____
3. _____
4. _____
5. _____

Number of Kids

1. _____
2. _____
3. _____
4. _____
5. _____

Future City

1. _____
2. _____
3. _____
4. _____
5. _____

Spiral Circle

Your Magic Number

CATEGORIES GAME

Letter	Country	Animal	Name	Job	City	Score

Number of Rounds

Total Score

DOTS AND BOXES

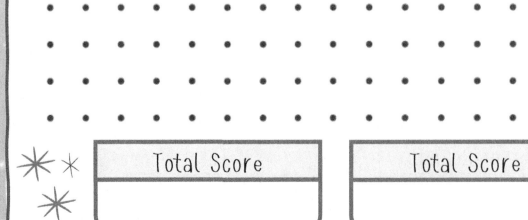

Total Score

Total Score

3D WEAVE MAZE #4

Start

Finish

FREE DRAW

Draw someone you look up to.

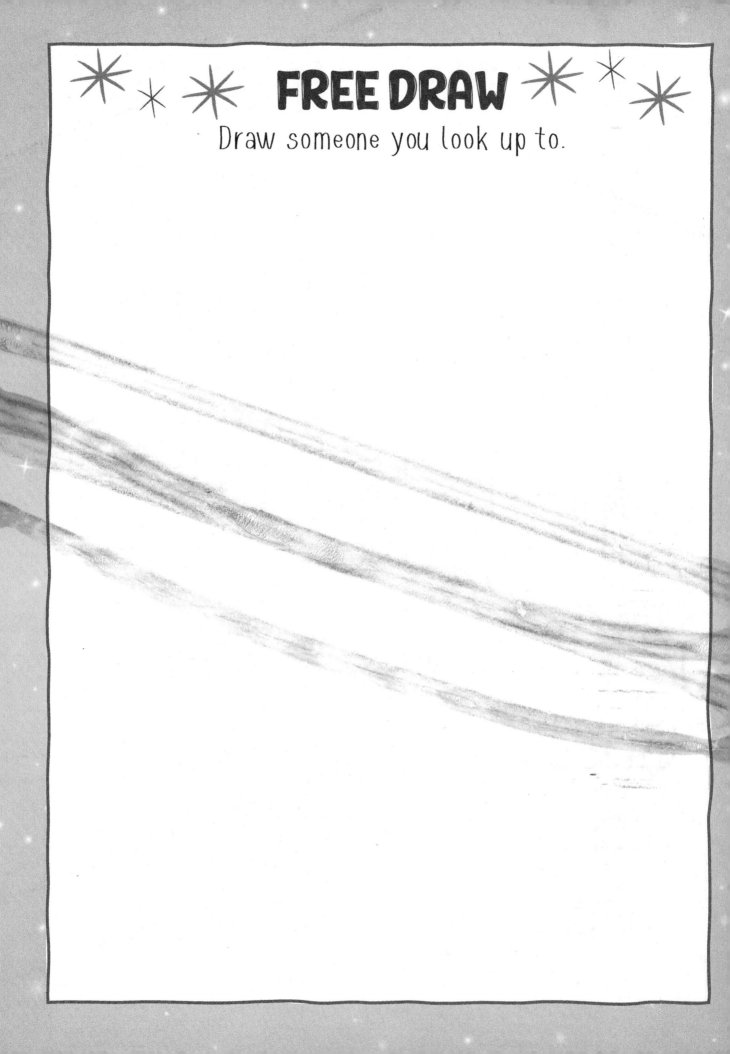

M.A.S.H.

MANSION-APARTMENT-SHACK-HOUSE

Future Spouse

1. _____
2. _____
3. _____
4. _____
5. _____

Future Pets

1. _____
2. _____
3. _____
4. _____
5. _____

Future Car

1. _____
2. _____
3. _____
4. _____
5. _____

Future Job

1. _____
2. _____
3. _____
4. _____
5. _____

Number of Kids

1. _____
2. _____
3. _____
4. _____
5. _____

Future City

1. _____
2. _____
3. _____
4. _____
5. _____

Spiral Circle

Your Magic Number

CATEGORIES GAME

Letter	Country	Animal	Name	Job	City	Score

Number of Rounds	Total Score

DOTS AND BOXES

Total Score	Total Score

FREE DRAW

Draw your future 5 years from now.

 # M.A.S.H.

MANSION-APARTMENT- SHACK-HOUSE

Future Spouse

1. _____
2. _____
3. _____
4. _____
5. _____

Future Pets

1. _____
2. _____
3. _____
4. _____
5. _____

Future Car

1. _____
2. _____
3. _____
4. _____
5. _____

Future Job

1. _____
2. _____
3. _____
4. _____
5. _____

Number of Kids

1. _____
2. _____
3. _____
4. _____
5. _____

Future City

1. _____
2. _____
3. _____
4. _____
5. _____

Spiral Circle

Your Magic Number

CATEGORIES GAME

Letter	Country	Animal	Name	Job	City	Score

Number of Rounds

Total Score

Puzzle 1 (top-left):

	2	6	1			5		
8	9							3
	4	1					7	
	3	9	5		7			1
5		2		1	6	3		
	7	4		6	3	9	2	
		8		1			6	4
4				6	7			9
	6	7		8		5		

Puzzle 2 (top-right):

		3			4			5
7		6	2			1	9	
4		5		9		7		8
		9		3	5		6	
		1		7				
		2	6				7	
		8	3	2	7	9		
3	6	7	8	4				2
2	9	4		6	1		8	

Puzzle 3 (bottom-left):

4								7
	3	8				9		
6				1			4	
	7	9		2			5	
2			5			1	6	
1		5			4	7	3	2
	4		9		5	8	1	
8	1	6		4	2		9	3
		3	1	8		7		

Puzzle 4 (bottom-right):

7						1		
1	9	3			4	2		8
5	6	8		3				9
	5	7	8	9	6	4	2	1
	1	6			3			
8	2	9	7	1		6		3
	7						6	2
			6	8	7			
				7				

M.A.S.H.

MANSION-APARTMENT- SHACK-HOUSE

Future Spouse

1. _____
2. _____
3. _____
4. _____
5. _____

Future Pets

1. _____
2. _____
3. _____
4. _____
5. _____

Future Car

1. _____
2. _____
3. _____
4. _____
5. _____

Future Job

1. _____
2. _____
3. _____
4. _____
5. _____

Number of Kids

1. _____
2. _____
3. _____
4. _____
5. _____

Future City

1. _____
2. _____
3. _____
4. _____
5. _____

Spiral Circle

Your Magic Number

DOTS AND BOXES

Total Score

Total Score

FREE DRAW
Draw something that you want.

# M.A.S.H.

MANSION-APARTMENT-SHACK-HOUSE

Future Spouse

1. _____
2. _____
3. _____
4. _____
5. _____

Future Pets

1. _____
2. _____
3. _____
4. _____
5. _____

Future Car

1. _____
2. _____
3. _____
4. _____
5. _____

Future Job

1. _____
2. _____
3. _____
4. _____
5. _____

Number of Kids

1. _____
2. _____
3. _____
4. _____
5. _____

Future City

1. _____
2. _____
3. _____
4. _____
5. _____

Spiral Circle

Your Magic Number

SOLUTiONS

EASY SOLUTIONS

8	6	4	9	3	7	5	2	1
1	5	3	4	6	2	8	7	9
2	7	9	5	8	1	4	6	3
5	3	1	8	2	6	7	9	4
9	2	7	3	4	5	1	8	6
6	4	8	7	1	9	2	3	5
3	1	2	6	7	4	9	5	8
4	8	5	2	9	3	6	1	7
7	9	6	1	5	8	3	4	2

7	5	9	6	4	2	1	3	8
8	2	6	1	3	5	7	9	4
1	3	4	8	9	7	6	2	5
4	9	3	5	6	1	2	8	7
5	6	7	3	2	8	9	4	1
2	8	1	4	7	9	5	6	3
6	7	5	9	8	4	3	1	2
3	4	2	7	1	6	8	5	9
9	1	8	2	5	3	4	7	6

6	2	3	5	1	9	4	8	7
5	4	9	2	7	8	3	6	1
8	1	7	6	4	3	9	2	5
7	3	2	1	5	6	8	9	4
9	8	1	4	3	7	2	5	6
4	5	6	8	9	2	1	7	3
3	9	4	7	8	5	6	1	2
1	6	5	9	2	4	7	3	8
2	7	8	3	6	1	5	4	9

5	6	4	9	3	1	7	8	2
8	1	9	6	2	7	3	5	4
7	3	2	4	8	5	1	6	9
1	8	7	2	9	4	5	3	6
3	9	6	5	1	8	2	4	7
2	4	5	7	6	3	8	9	1
9	5	8	1	4	2	6	7	3
4	7	1	3	5	6	9	2	8
6	2	3	8	7	9	4	1	5

MEDIUM SOLUTIONS

Grid 1

7	1	8	3	6	9	4	5	2
6	2	5	1	4	7	9	8	3
9	3	4	2	8	5	7	1	6
4	9	1	5	3	2	6	7	8
3	6	7	4	9	8	1	2	5
5	8	2	6	7	1	3	9	4
2	5	6	9	1	3	8	4	7
1	7	3	8	5	4	2	6	9
8	4	9	7	2	6	5	3	1

Grid 2

9	4	3	1	6	8	7	5	2
5	7	8	2	3	9	1	4	6
2	6	1	5	7	4	3	8	9
8	1	5	6	9	2	4	7	3
7	2	9	4	1	3	8	6	5
6	3	4	7	8	5	9	2	1
3	9	6	8	5	7	2	1	4
4	5	7	3	2	1	6	9	8
1	8	2	9	4	6	5	3	7

Grid 3

9	6	7	3	5	8	2	4	1
3	1	4	9	6	2	8	5	7
8	5	2	4	1	7	3	9	6
2	9	1	8	7	4	6	3	5
5	4	6	1	2	3	9	7	8
7	3	8	6	9	5	4	1	2
1	8	3	5	4	6	7	2	9
6	7	5	2	3	9	1	8	4
4	2	9	7	8	1	5	6	3

Grid 4

2	6	7	5	1	3	8	9	4
9	5	3	2	8	4	1	7	6
8	4	1	9	6	7	2	3	5
4	1	9	6	2	8	3	5	7
3	2	5	4	7	1	9	6	8
6	7	8	3	5	9	4	1	2
5	8	2	1	9	6	7	4	3
7	9	4	8	3	5	6	2	1
1	3	6	7	4	2	5	8	9

HARD SOLUTIONS

7	2	6	1	3	4	5	9	8
8	9	5	6	7	2	4	1	3
3	4	1	9	8	5	2	7	6
6	3	9	5	2	7	8	4	1
5	8	2	4	9	1	6	3	7
1	7	4	8	6	3	9	2	5
2	5	8	7	1	9	3	6	4
4	1	3	2	5	6	7	8	9
9	6	7	3	4	8	1	5	2

9	1	3	7	8	4	6	2	5
7	8	6	2	5	3	1	9	4
4	2	5	1	9	6	7	3	8
8	7	9	4	3	5	2	6	1
6	4	1	9	7	2	8	5	3
5	3	2	6	1	8	4	7	9
1	5	8	3	2	7	9	4	6
3	6	7	8	4	9	5	1	2
2	9	4	5	6	1	3	8	7

4	2	1	3	5	9	6	8	7
5	3	8	4	6	7	9	2	1
6	9	7	2	1	8	3	4	5
3	7	9	6	2	1	4	5	8
2	8	4	5	7	3	1	6	9
1	6	5	8	9	4	7	3	2
7	4	2	9	3	5	8	1	6
8	1	6	7	4	2	5	9	3
9	5	3	1	8	6	2	7	4

7	4	2	9	8	5	1	3	6
1	9	3	6	4	2	5	7	8
5	6	8	1	3	7	2	4	9
3	5	7	8	9	6	4	2	1
4	1	6	5	2	3	9	8	7
8	2	9	7	1	4	6	5	3
9	7	4	3	5	1	8	6	2
2	3	1	4	6	8	7	9	5
6	8	5	2	7	9	3	1	4

3D WEAVE MAZES

#1

#2

#3

#4

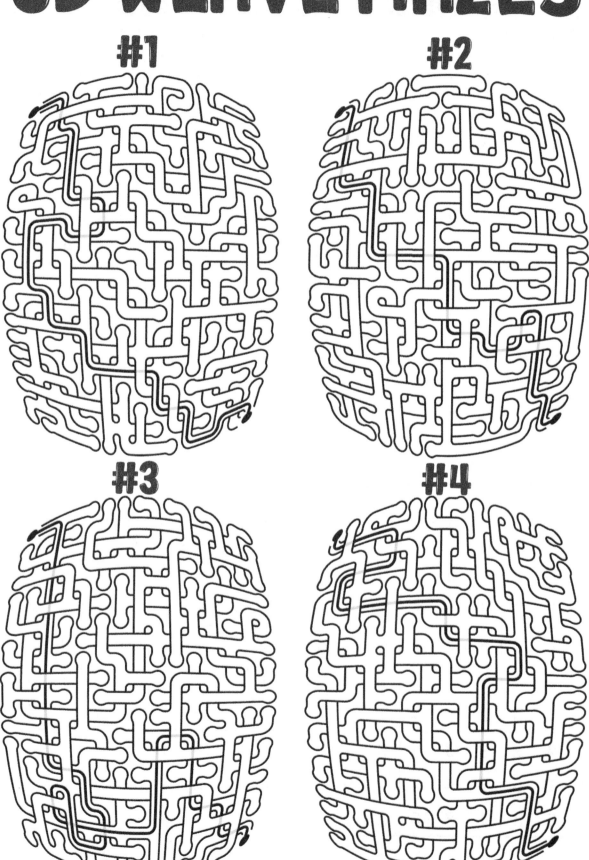

Made in the USA
Monee, IL
17 April 2023

30495115R00057